Soul Food
31 Day Devotional
By Gregory J. Williams

ISBN 9 7 8 - 6 2 1 - 9 6 4 2 0 - 1 - 9

Daily Devotional

Gregory J Williams

Daily Devotions for your Soul.

Pause,

Meditate,

Pray.

Pause:

To temporary stop in action or speech. To cease from your regular daily routine to spend some time with God.

Meditate:

To focus one's mind for a period of time, in silence and to think deeply. To reflect on God's word and allow His word to shape your life.

Pray:

To make earnest petition. To have a conversation with God.

1

Joshua 1:8

Our success in life is dependent on our knowledge of God's word. That is what God says to Joshua as he is about to cross Jordan into the promised land.

We pay attention to a lot of things in our world. Friends, social media and television shows among other things. We often follow what popular celebrities are doing or wearing or using. While it might be fascinating, it does not have the power to transform your life.

'Keep this Book of the Law always on your lips; meditate on it day and night, so that you may be careful to do everything written in it. Then you will be prosperous and successful. '

Joshua 1:8

Only God's word has the power to change our lives for the better. Not only does God tell Joshua to meditate on the word but He shares an important benefit of doing that.

Our success and prosperity in life is directly tied to reading and obeying God's wisdom.

Early in my walk of faith I learnt the importance of honouring God's word. The more I paid attention to it, the more I saw good things happen in my life.

I have found promises and comfort, healing, life and wisdom in His word. As God's word begins to shape our lives it begins to provide us with ways to live a life of success.

Meditate on what His word says today, Pray His word into your life and you will see the amazing benefits of His word

Take a few minutes to pause, mediate and pray.

2

Psalm 119:105-106

I try to walk as often as I can and on this particular afternoon I decided to take a new path, one that I was unfamiliar with and had never been down before. It was an enjoyable meandering walkway next to a small brook and I got caught up in admiring the scenery and pretty soon I was lost. I was unsure of where I ended up and there were no familiar signs to show me a way out. Thankfully I had my phone with me and a quick check of the map helped me navigate my way out.

As I walked back to familiar grounds I could not help but think about the words in the Psalms

'Your word is a lamp for my feet, a light on my path. I have taken an oath and confirmed it, that I will follow your righteous laws. '

Psalms 119:105-106

God's word helps us illuminate our path in life. Sometimes we get distracted by the sights and sounds around us and wander off the path He has laid down for us. I know in my life, just like on my walk I have often taken a path that had me lost in life. It has always been God's word, like a GPS that has helped me find my path again. When we are lost, unsure, hesitant and disheartened, it's God's truth and firm word that help us navigate back to familiar and safe places in His presence.

The Psalmist says that His word is beam of hope in dark times. A flashlight does not light up everything around us. It helps shine light on the path before us so we don't stumble, fall and injure ourselves. It shows us a clear path in front of us. A light on our path in life.

This is what God's word does for us. It helps us shine a light on the path before us and enables us to navigate though life. It helps us see clearly the road ahead of us. It leads us out of darkness and into His light.

Where are you on your journey today? Do you need to find your way back? Have you got your flashlight shining on the path before you?

Wherever you are on your journey it's always wise to invite God to help guide you further in life.

Take a few minutes to pause, mediate and pray.

3

Philippians 3:13-14

One of the highlights of the Olympic Games is the 100 meters. It determines the fastest human on the planet and it is the glamour event of the Olympics. It's over in less than 10 seconds but it draws so much attention. The crowd roars, as the runners shoot out of the blocks. People are glued to their televisions across the world. Nations hoping their athlete wins the ultimate glory.

The runners however are so focused they don't hear the crowd or observe the television cameras or see the stadium packed with people. Their focus is on the finish line.

When the race starts the competitors are unconcerned with what is behind them. It's just what's in front of them that matters.

Paul brings this thought into our relationship with Christ. We live in busy worlds with lots going on. There is the constant roar of distraction. Our mobile devices are constantly demanding our attention and our focus moves from one thing to another so quickly.

What Paul, the great apostle, is encouraging us to do, is to not eliminate everything from our life, but to focus in on what's really important: God's will for each of us.

We cannot change our environment or our surroundings but we can choose to focus on something. To make an intentional choice for our own good.

He says

'Brothers and sisters, I do not consider myself yet to have taken hold of it. But one thing I do: Forgetting what is behind and straining toward what is ahead, I press on toward the goal to win the prize for which God has called me heavenward in Christ Jesus. '

Philippians 3:13-14

Our prize is Christ and He is our reward. When we choose to focus on Him, there is immeasurable peace and joy that will fill our world.

So choose in your world to focus on what is really important, something that can help you in your life: Your relationship with Jesus.

Take a few minutes to pause, mediate and pray.

4

Jeremiah 29:11

Before we ever set foot into our new home, we knew what it would look like. We knew the size of each room and what the floor would look like and what the doors and ceiling would look like. The reason we did, was because we had gone to see a display home and also had the opportunity to sit with the home designer who showed us the blueprints and pictures of what the colours and floorpan of the house would look like.

However, when we did walk into our home there was still a sense of great joy to see that the plans had come to fruition. There is nothing like touching and walking though the real thing.

Much like that, God has so many amazing plans for us and He tells us so in His word and in our private time with Him.

He speaks of the future plans He has for us. How he plans to bless us and provide for us and protect us.

'For I know the plans I have for you," declares the Lord , "plans to prosper you and not to harm you, plans to give you hope and a future. '

Jeremiah 29:11

Before you were even born, God purposefully prepared plans just for you. Not generic or mass plans for everyone, but individually catered plans just for you.

Lovingly crafted with you in mind. Each one amazing and specific, designed just for you. As we move through our lives each one is unveiled in its beauty.

Sometimes we see a glimpse of them far ahead of us, and we can appreciate the meticulous planning that He does for us. However, there is nothing like those plans actually materialising in our lives. Much like walking though a house where you can touch and feel, there is another level of joy that comes into our lives.

Reflect on the fact that each plan God has put in place, if you follow His leading, will certainly come to pass. Talk to Him today about some of those amazing plans He has for you.

Take a few minutes to pause, mediate and pray.

5

Isaiah 40:31

Watching an eagle soar is mesmerising, it floats effortless on the broad span of its majestic wings. The wind currents help it gain altitude and from its high vantage point it can clearly see its intended target, often hundreds of feet below.

The eagle does not spend a lot of energy flapping its wings like other birds to stay aloft, but maintains its flight because of the updrafts. This wind is the key to the soaring of an eagle.

Our hope in God's promises gives us the ability to also remain aloft in troubled times. It is reported that when storms roll into the eagles territory it will often soar above the storm, high above the clouds and rain, thus not being affected by the inclement weather.

When we allow God's word to elevate us, we gain a whole new perspective on our problems. When we rely on His word to help us navigate though life, we do indeed get the ability to renew our strength and soar above the issues we face. It's not that the problem disappears, but rather we gain a new perspective on the things we face.

'But those who hope in the Lord will renew their strength. They will soar on wings like eagles; they will run and not grow weary, they will walk and not be faint.'

Isaiah 40:31

God's word renews and refreshes us. It reinvigorates us with hope. When we continue to believe His word it empowers us to remain positive and hopeful in difficult seasons.

What are you going through today where you need God's word to give you hope? Put your trust in Him. He will help you soar like an eagle over your problems.

Take a few minutes to pause, mediate and pray.

6

Psalms 5:11

Getting caught in the rain with no umbrella is not a fun experience, especially when you are wearing your good clothes.

We look for the closest building or shelter to run under so we can get out of the downpour. We realise that it can protect us from the sudden cloudburst.

What about the sudden downpours of crisis in our lives? All of us at some point come to the place where we are hit by something we did not foresee or anticipate. We want to duck and hide or run for cover. Unfortunately, it often feels like we cannot escape the downpour.

It's at these times we really need sound advice to help us navigate our way out of the crisis. We all need a place where we can feel loved and protected.

The psalmist points us in the direction where, regardless of our circumstances, we can find a place of protection and refuge.

'But let all who take refuge in you be glad; let them ever sing for joy. Spread your protection over them, that those who love your name may rejoice in you. '

Psalms 5:11

To take refuge means to be in a state of being safe or sheltered from pursuit, danger, or difficulty. God offers guidance, comfort, peace and joy when we seek Him out in our difficult seasons. In Him we find protection and the solution to our problems.

What have you found difficult in your week? Do you need a place where you are loved and protected? Invite God into your circumstances today and let Him protect you from your storm.

Take a few minutes to pause, mediate and pray.

7

Deuteronomy 31:6

When I was a child I was often bullied in school. It made me feel insignificant and weak. I remember wishing that I had an older bother who could come and defend me. The trouble was, I was the eldest child and there would never be an older sibling who would ever come to my defense.

At some point in our lives we feel intimidated by others. Some look down on us, pick on us and make fun of us. No one is immune from such horrible behaviour. Some may be physically strong but even that does not leave them immune to harassment or peer pressure.

When we look at the world around us there is always something that makes us feel inferior or intimidated. There will not aways be someone to defend us. Sometimes even those closest to us may not be able to help.

However, God is always there to be our helper. He can and will be there in all situations in our life. There will never be a time when God cannot help. So rather than looking at the size of our problem, let us fix our attention on the size of our God.

Our God is the most powerful force in existence and He has never been defeated. When He is at our side, we are able to dispel fear and be courageous.

'Be strong and courageous. Do not be afraid or terrified because of them, for the Lord your God goes with you; he will never leave you nor forsake you." '

Deuteronomy 31:6

What is causing you to be fearful? Fear can often cripple us. We all need a someone who will be there in difficult times. God assures us that He is the One who will be with us wherever we go.

Ask Him to remove fear and remind yourself that He is always with you.

Take a few minutes to pause, mediate and pray.

8

Isaiah 26:3-4

Have you ever been in a scary situation? I have been in the middle of a huge earthquake and it was scary! A host of thoughts run through your mind, the prevailing thought being: Will I survive?

One of the most stressful things of being in an earthquake is not just when it happens, but the anticipation of when it will occur again. There were a number of aftershocks and a couple of more earthquakes before things calmed down for a bit.

You are constantly thinking about where you could be when the earthquake hits and hyper aware of potential exits especially if you are in a building. You don't want to be in a structure of any kind when an earthquake hits, in case it comes down on you.

Even sleeping is difficult because you never know when it might hit again. It was in the middle of this that I focused on God's peace.

It's in the difficult situations of life that we need to have something to hope for. It's in the lack of something that we truly appreciate its value. When we are extremely thirsty we really want a drink of water. At other times even though it might be all around us we don't pay much attention to it.

It is when we are in stress and disputes and strife that we long for peace. A place to gather our thoughts and feelings.

Like me I am sure you have many situations where you long for peace. You might not be in an earthquake, but sometimes it feels like our whole world is shaking from all of the things that come into it.

'Trust in the Lord forever, for the Lord , the Lord himself, is the Rock eternal. You will keep in perfect peace those whose minds are steadfast, because they trust in you. '

Isaiah 26:3-4

Even in the middle of the most stress inducing situations God will flood you with His peace, if you put your trust in Him. The more I leaned into God's peace the lower my anxiety became.

What are you going thought in your life where you need God's peace?

Where do you need His peace in your life? Lean into God today and put your trust in Him and He will lead you through.

Take a few minutes to pause, mediate and pray.

9

Romans 8:28

I have often questioned why certain things have happened to me. When bad things come into my life. I asked God why?

None of us like to be disappointed, rejected, let down or betrayed but all of us have felt the sting of those experiences. I've had one of my closest friends steal money from me and I know the hurt that comes from discovering that. Negative things happen in the world we live in and sometimes it feels like there is no rhyme or reason for things to happen. When we don't understand we question and that is quite normal.

God, however, does not look with the same lens that we do. His view is not constrained by time or space or limited to the here and now. He sees beyond the present.

He understands the anguish we sometimes face and He comforts us through it. More importantly, He will use every experience to teach us a valuable lesson. As any loving father guides his child, more so will God guide us. He does not bring bad things into our life. We live in a world of free choice and often evil people make evil choices.

What God uniquely does, that no one else can do is that He takes all of our bad experiences and turns them into something good.

'And we know that in all things God works for the good of those who love him, who have been called according to his purpose. '

Romans 8:28

Having money stolen from a friend I trusted was not good. But having God show me how to forgive in spite of the pain was good. If God can forgive my sin which was far worse than stealing money, then I can forgive others who mistreat me.

What are you holding onto that you feel that you have been unfairly treated? Do you struggle with letting some things go?

God will help turn our pain in rejoicing. All we have to do is take it to Him. Whatever you are going though bring it to Him, and place it at His feet and leave it there.

Take a few minutes to pause, mediate and pray.

10

Philippians 4:6-7

I was stuck in traffic and in danger of missing my flight. I was anxious and trying to will the traffic to move. But of course nothing happened. Cars don't move because I want them to or care if I miss my flight.

It's easy to get stressed about things we cannot control. It's not so easy to try to stop being anxious. When we look at what is going wrong or what could go wrong the natural inclination is to panic. However, we must know that being stressed or anxious or flying into a panic can in no way change the situation we are in.

Nothing will change because of our level of anxiety. In fact what happens is that we cause ourselves to go deeper into irrational emotion.

God always provides us with a solution when we seem to run off the track with our emotions. His advice is simple. No matter the situation, no matter the circumstance bring it to Him in prayer.

Siting in the car and realising that I don't control the traffic and being anxious was pointless: rather I turned my attention to Christ. I asked for His peace to fill the car and my life. Almost immediately my anxiety began to ease.

'Do not be anxious about anything, but in every situation, by prayer and petition, with thanksgiving, present your requests to God. And the peace of God, which transcends all understanding, will guard your hearts and your minds in Christ Jesus. '

Philippians 4:6-7

I did eventually make it to the airport, and arriving in a less than an anxious state helped me navigate quickly though the checks and onto the plane on time.

Even when things don't go the way we want, anxiety never helps us. What are you anxious about? What is casing you to feel tense. Bring it to God in prayer and He will give you transcendent peace in exchange.

Take a few minutes to pause, mediate and pray.

11

James 1:12

As a teenager learning to drive is the ultimate ticket to freedom. No longer would I have to beg and plead to be driven to and from the places I wanted to go or resort to the long arduous journey of public transportation. To get that drivers license in my hand was going to be the best feeling. Standing in front of me obtaining that said drivers license was a scowling government employee who looked like he was in no mood to allow even the most skilled race car driver loose on "his" roads.

I had to prove to him beyond a shadow of doubt that I could pass his test. Of course I failed.

I had to go back in a few weeks and this time I managed to pass. What motivated me to go back after the initial disappointment was the promise of freedom the driver's licence provided. The test was just the obstacle that I needed to get past to obtain what I wanted.

If we look at the problems in front of us we often feel deflated and discouraged. All too often we focus on what the test is, the trial is, the problem is. We don't see the result. And when we focus on the wrong thing our motivation wanes.

'Blessed is the one who perseveres under trial because, having stood the test, that person will receive the crown of life that the Lord has promised to those who love him. '

James 1:12

There is something beyond the trial you are facing, the blessing you will receive when you come though it. When we lose sight of it the task becomes monotonous. When we see what we will gain, the task just becomes what we need to go though to get it. The reward motivates us forward.

What do you see in your life that feels like a test? Ask God to show you the benefit, Look at the opportunity and not the obstacle.

Take a few minutes to pause, mediate and pray.

12

2 Corinthians 5:17

I love T-shirts and getting a new one, especially with a great new print has always been exciting. However, I have a bad habit of not getting rid of the old T-shirts I have. Some of them are way past the use by date. There are tears and holes in some, and I always make the excuse of saying maybe I can use them around the house.

The old ones take up space in my closet and to be honest I rarely use them. Yet they occupy a shelf I could use to put clothes I actually wear.

God has given us a new a new life. When we become Christ followers we become a new creation. However, we like to hang on to things from the past. Old behaviour or proclivities tie us to our old shelves, and they hang around (like my old T-shirts) taking up space and attention in our lives.

'Therefore, if anyone is in Christ, the new creation has come: The old has gone, the new is here!

'2 Corinthians 5:17

We need to remind ourselves that Christ has made us new and with this new life we can make new choices to walk in alignment with our new nature. We must decide to put away old habits and behaviour that tarnish the image God has created us in.

Our choices must reflect our new nature, not pull us into our former nature.

Remember you are a child of God who has been bought with a price. You are called to be a reflection of His image

What habits do you need to purge from your life? Ask God to help establish His character in you and put away old things.

Take a few minutes to pause, mediate and pray.

13

Hebrews 11:1

Fear paralyses us, but faith releases us into the place God has for us. How many times has fear stopped you from stepping out and experiencing something important?

Faith is not just a warm fuzzy feeling you get when you think about God. It's being supremely confident in the nature of who God is. In essence it means trusting what God says is true. Faith is not believing for what I want and then asking God for it and saying: "If I believe strongly enough it will happen."

Faith in God is trusting that He will do what is best for us and give us what He thinks is necessary for us. It's trusting Him even when our current surroundings don't necessarily reflect what we want to happen.

God is not a genie in a bottle. We can't ask for something we want and expect God to perform to our wish. He is not there to grant our wishes. Faith in God says: Lord, I trust you more than anything and I know you will do what's best for me

Faith is putting hope and assurance in a God who cannot fail.

'Now faith is confidence in what we hope for and assurance about what we do not see. '

Hebrews 11:1

To strengthen our faith we need to read God's word and start to trust in it. We don't base our faith on what we see but on what God's word says in spite of what we actually see.

What are you struggling with today? Where do you need to stretch your faith? Ask God to show you His word in a new light so you establish your faith on His word and His promises

Take a few minutes to pause, mediate and pray.

14

Matthew 17:20

What bad habits do you have? It seems we all have a collection of bad or unhealthy habits and they are so hard to get rid of. It's commonly said that if you do something for 4 weeks consistently you will develop a new habit. While we have to make a effort to incorporate good things into our regime, we often don't have to try hard at all to adopt bad habits.

Paul, the great apostle wants to inform and remind us that God gave us the ability to be self-disciplined and it benefits us to implement good and productive habits into out lives.

As Christ followers we are created in the image of God and thus we have been imputed with the nature of Jesus, so we can have the qualities that come with that nature.

'For the Spirit God gave us does not make us timid, but gives us power, love and self-discipline.

'2 Timothy 1:7

What area of your life do you feel you need to do more? Is it praying more? Reading your Bible? Being encouraging to those around you?

We don’t need to be timid, that does not come from God, but let's be courageous in stepping out on a new journey to make ourselves more in line with what our true nature is.

Ask God to help give you more of His power, and accept His love. Resolve to be more self disciplined in your life.

Take a few minutes to pause, mediate and pray.

15

2 Timothy 1:7

When we feel something is just too hard we throw up our hands in resignation and say : "It's impossible!" I remember going to watch a basketball game and in the last few minutes of the game our home team was down too many points. It looked almost impossible for them to come back and win. So my friend and I decided to leave and avoid the massive crowd at the end of the game. When we got to our car we turned on the radio only to be shocked to learn the team had come roaring back and were only down by two points. In the last few seconds of the game they scored a basket and eventually won! We were both excited and disappointed at the same time. Excited that our team won and disappointed that we had not stayed to witness it.

Ive heard it said "Impossible" is just a word but did you know the word impossible actually says "I'm Possible"!

All too often we give up before even trying or trusting God.

Jesus's words here encourage us to have faith, a little faith can do a whole lot He says:

'He replied, "Because you have so little faith. Truly I tell you, if you have faith as small as a mustard seed, you can say to this mountain, 'Move from here to there,' and it will move. Nothing will be impossible for you."

Matthew 17:20

Before we throw our hands up in surrender too quickly, lets pause and examine the situation. More importantly lets pray and invite God into the circumstance. Let Him have the final say.

What "impossible" situation can you invite God into today?

Take a few minutes to pause, mediate and pray.

16

Lamentations 3:22-23

I've been through a period of my life when I just did not feel like waking up, or getting out of bed. I was going through depression and pain and I was feeling very sorry for myself. All I could see was what people had done to me and I did not feel it was right or fair.

I'm sure that you have also felt unfairly treated at some point in your life. Maybe it was someone who betrayed you or took advantage of you or even made you feel unloved. When we look at what we lost there is much cause for anguish. It's when we start to look beyond ourselves that we gain perspective.

In spite of my feelings, God's love and comfort woke me up each morning. It's when I began to shift my attention from me to Him that I began to emerge from my depression.

Each morning God displays His love for us by giving us breath and strength and mercy and goodness. God has been faithful to us, even when we have not been faithful to Him.

He is generous with His love. When I started to look at His love and experience His compassion I began to throw off the mist of depression.

'Because of the Lord's great love we are not consumed, for his compassions never fail. They are new every morning; great is your faithfulness. '

Lamentations 3:22-23

Rather than look at what people have done to us, let's look at what the Lord does for us. He is always there to comfort and guide us through even the most difficult times of our lives

Turn your attention to God's love and presence. Rather than focus on what you have lost, look at much you gain when you experience His love. In which area of your life do you need His love the most today?

Take a few minutes to pause, mediate and pray.

17

Proverbs 18:10

I was sitting on a bench and noticed a father playing with his young daughter. The little girl was quite adventurous as she ran around the little park. Her father kept a close eye on her. Excited she skipped and jumped around and called to her father to watch her as she performed these activities. Her father, a broad smile stretched across his face, encouraged her and clapped at everything she did. He was just as excited as she was.

Then disaster! She tripped and fell, bruising her little knees. Tears started streaming down her face and she reach to her father crying " Daddy" Almost instantly her father swooped down and gathered her up into his arms comforting her.

I recall thinking this exactly how it is with our heavenly Father. When we stumble and fall we can call out to Him and he comes and lifts us into his safe arms.

'The name of the Lord is a fortified tower; the righteous run to it and are safe. '

Proverbs 18:10

Our God is a good Father, who cares for His children. He watches us with loving eyes. He pays close attention to us and we are never out of His sight.

All we have to do is call out to Him in a time of need and He is right there. His name, the scriptures says is a strong tower. We can always run to Him and find safety from whatever seeks to harm us.

What do you need comfort in today? Run into His arms to find comfort and love

Take a few minutes to pause, mediate and pray.

18

Romans 15:13

I was pouring myself a cup of tea and for a moment I got distracted, I overfilled my cup and the tea flowed over onto the table. As I was cleaning up the table I began to think about what God means when He says that I may overflow with hope.

When something overflows a cup or a bottle or even a river it means that what you are trying to put into a container exceeds what it's able to bear or carry and so it spills over.

'May the God of hope fill you with all joy and peace as you trust in him, so that you may overflow with hope by the power of the Holy Spirit. '

Romans 15:13

There are many areas in life where we don't want more that we can bear. Hope is not one of those things. We all need more of it in our lives. God desires to pour inexhaustible quantities of hope and joy and peace into our lives constantly, so that we can have more than we can possibly require. Hope helps us fix our eyes on a better future. A place that lies before us, where we have come past the pain and the hurt of disappointment.

When we put our trust in Him, He pours hope into our life, so much hope, that it bursts over our life and overflows our heart. It fills our whole being so we can lift our eyes from our current situation and see a place where we are free from the angst of the thing that is causing us distress.

What are you struggling with that makes you feel hopeless? Turn your thoughts and prayers to Jesus and let the promise of His hope, peace and joy flood over you and explode in your heart.

What concern or worry are you struggling with today? Bring your cares to Him and exchange it for His hope

Take a few minutes to pause, mediate and pray.

19

Psalms 116:1-2

When a baby cries its mother instinctively responds. Ive seen mothers recognise the cry of their baby even when there are a number of other babies that may also be crying in the same room. They have learned to distinguish their baby's cry from others.

Our Father, who knows our voices and loves us so overwhelmingly, can discern our individual cry from others and He will always hear us. No matter where we are or what situation we find ourselves in, our God is always able to hear us when we call on Him.

I've been though some dark seasons in my life while others have brought me great joy, but regardless of the circumstances around me, whenever I call on the name of the Lord, He has always heard me.

I love the Lord , for he heard my voice; he heard my cry for mercy. Because he turned his ear to me, I will call on him as long as I live. '

Psalms 116:1-2

It's in times of difficulty that we call out for help. It's in these times we need to be heard. The Psalmist assures us that, when he calls, God hears.

He hears our prayers, He hears our cries of pain and our cries for help. He is an ever present God who will not leave us when we need Him. He will not abandon us when we call out to Him. Regardless of what we are going though, He is faithful to us.

It's because of this faithfulness that the writer says I will call on Him all of my life. He, like us can be confident that our God will always be present in our lives.

What do you need to call on God for today?

Take a few minutes to pause, mediate and pray.

20

Psalms 55:22

As a child I made a small bridge over a tiny stream in our back yard. It was not more than a foot across and a flat piece of a discarded tree branch served as the bridge. I wanted to help the ants get across. I then thought I would add more things to the tiny bridge, a few more leaves and a stone to help weigh it down and stop it from blowing away. However, soon enough the tiny bridge buckled under the weight of the things I had heaped on it and it broke. I had to find another branch and start again.

Often we carry a whole lot of trouble and cares and it becomes something that will eventually break us or wear us down. No matter how strong we think we are, we all have a breaking point. That old adage of "the last straw breaking the camels back" is very true.

The truth is that we don't have to carry our burdens by ourselves. We can unburden ourselves if we choose to. We can shift them to God who is able to bear the weight of our concerns. The word cast means to "throw" and its an act of relieving ourselves of the weight, when we "throw" them on the Lord.

'Cast your cares on the Lord and he will sustain you; he will never let the righteous be shaken. '

Psalms 55:22

When we do unburden ourselves from the weight of cares and troubles, it helps us become better equipped to function at greater efficiency.

God encourages us to move burdens from ourselves to Him because He knows what carrying the weight all of that will do to us. He does not want us to buckle, He wants to uplift and sustain us.

So how much we carry is totally up to us. Why carry anything at all? Cast your cares upon Him for He cares for you.

Take a few minutes to pause, mediate and pray.

21

Habakkuk 3:19

I was enthralled watching mountain goats jump from what looked like sheer cliff faces to almost imperceptible footholds on the mountain. The documentary spoke of how surefooted these creatures are when they traverse the hard terrain. As the camera pulled back to show this massive drop, the white goat look like a speck against the majesty of the mountain.

These wonderful creatures are so skilled and surefooted they make this treacherous act look common place. Yet it's fraught with dangers and deadly drops. One little mistake was all it would take for the goat to plunge to its death several hundred feet to the bottom. It's sheer confidence and skill kept this from happening.

'The Sovereign Lord is my strength; he makes my feet like the feet of a deer, he enables me to tread on the heights.

Habakkuk 3:19

When we invite God into our daily walk He can help us navigate the pitfalls of our journey. There are many pitfalls that we can encounter in life and with the Lord's wise counsel we are able to go from one strong foothold to another.

Like you, I don't want to end up in disaster from poor decisions and the best way to avoid that is to seek God's guidance in all our decisions. When we seek Him, not just in big situations in our life, but in every decision, big or small we are better equipped to go from strength to strength.

What big decision are you facing? Invite Him to give you His wisdom in every situation and you will find that you will achieve better success in your life.

Take a few minutes to pause, mediate and pray.

22

Philippians 1:4-6

Michelangelo, one of history's greatest sculptors understood the art of creating something beautiful. It is reported he said: “Every block of stone has a statue inside it and it is the task of the sculptor to discover it. I saw the angel in the marble and carved until I set him free.”

He is basically saying that when he looks at a piece of rough marble he sees the form in it and that he works with patience and care to bring what he sees on the inside, out.

God who is infinitely more skilled than Michelangelo does a creative work in our lives. He works taking off some of the sharp edges, He’s sanding down some of the rough bits, shaping up some other places and perfecting others and all of this is being done though the experiences in our lives.

In all my prayers for all of you, I always pray with joy because of your partnership in the gospel from the first day until now, being confident of this, that he who began a good work in you will carry it on to completion until the day of Christ Jesus. ‘

Philippians 1:4-6

You are God's wonderful creation. As God sculpts His masterpiece He uses each experience to help make us into the person He has desires us to become.

The one thing we can be sure of is that God has not abandoned us or forgotten us. We have not been absent from His mind, even for a second. He started something and He will complete it. All of us are masterpieces in progress. God is still sculpting, still painting, still working on us and through us.

What are you going through that you find difficult? Look with fresh eyes to how God is forming His character in you.

Take a few minutes to pause, mediate and pray.

23

1 Corinthians 16:13-14

I was watching a friend build a deck in his back yard. The first thing he did was dig deep holes for the posts to go in. He then put the wooden posts in and poured concrete around them to secure them in place to make sure they held firm and were strong enough to hold the weight of the deck. They had to be strong enough to hold the people who would sit upon it. That deck was solid and firm and even though a number of people stood on it it did not shake or give.

When we build structures especially buildings we want them to have the strength and construction integrity to withstand pressure from daily use and stand the test of time, plus a number of other external factors like extreme weather.

All sturdy structures have a solid foundation to hold them firm. To build high you first have to go down and construct a solid foundation.

In like fashion, we need to build strong foundations with our faith in God. We have to be able to withstand the storms of life and all of the other things that get thrown our way.

'Be on your guard; stand firm in the faith; be courageous; be strong. Do everything in love. '

1 Corinthians 16:13-14

The strength of our faith comes from taking God at His word and believing that He is who He says He is and that He will do what He said He will do. Our faith is a key ingredient in the construction of our lives and when we have strong faith we are able to withstand the pressures that life brings.

Build your firm foundation by reading and applying God's promises in your life. How can today's scripture help you do that?

Take a few minutes to pause, mediate and pray.

24

Hebrews 12:1-2

When I was in school my friends and I used to spend our breaks racing around the school building. We always got thrills from seeing who was the fastest. It always came down to one particular friend and myself who were always competing for first place.

The key to winning was keeping focused on the finish line and not being distracted by anything around us. Even glancing at where my rival was would throw off my rhythm and slow me down.

The triumph was in wining, getting to the finish line first. It did not matter how close or far my competitors were if I could get to the finish line first. Keeping my eye on the finish line helped me run a more efficient race.

Keeping our eyes on Jesus enables us to have a more efficient life as a Christ follower. The writer says the there is joy in what Christ saw before Him, even though what was there was the torture and agony of the cross. It was the joy of knowing that He would be able to reconcile all of us to God, and that was a wonderful thing.

'Therefore, since we are surrounded by such a great cloud of witnesses, let us throw off everything that hinders and the sin that so easily entangles. And let us run with perseverance the race marked out for us, fixing our eyes on Jesus, the pioneer and perfecter of faith. For the joy set before him he endured the cross, scorning its shame, and sat down at the right hand of the throne of God. '

Hebrews 12:1-2

Let us also not be distracted from our walk with the Lord. There is great joy that comes from a lasting and enduring relationship with Jesus. We can be assured that no matter what we go through, we can find comfort, security and love in His presence. So let's keep focused on Him and not on all of the other things that can ruin our relationship with God.

Where do you find yourself being distracted? When do you need to fix your eyes on Him?

Take a few minutes to pause, mediate and pray.

25

Nehemiah 2:4-5

When I make quick impromptu decisions or impulse choices I often find I have deep regrets. Most recently I rushed out and bought a TV because it was on sale and less than a year later I had problems with it. When we make uninformed decisions we get ourselves into problems. When we don't invite God in, before we make decisions, we make foolish choices and have severe regrets.

I have learnt that no decision is too big or small to have God involved in the process. We should get into the habit of praying before we make any choices. After all God knowswhat's best for us even when we don't. It does not have to be a long, lengthy prayer. I often pray what I call microwave prayers: "Lord help me please!"

'The king said to me, "What is it you want?" Then I prayed to the God of heaven, and I answered the king, "If it pleases the king and if your servant has found favour in his sight, let him send me to the city in Judah where my ancestors are buried so that I can rebuild it."

Nehemiah 2:4-5

Nehemiah had a heavy burden for his ancestral home that lay in ruins. When the king of Babylon, whom he served asked him what he wanted, Nehemiah prayed before he answered. Then he asked the King for what he wanted. The King gave him whatever he asked for, even though what he asked for was outrageous.

When we do consult God before answering or making a decision it enables us to make better choices. His guidance can prevent a lot of negative things impacting us.

Make it a regular habit to invite God into any big or small decisions that you have in your life and you will notice the trajectory of your life will take you to a better place.

What decision can you pray about today?

Take a few minutes to pause, mediate and pray.

26

Revelation 3:20

My wife and I enjoy the company of our friends and when they do come over for a meal, we have a great time chatting and catching up on signifiant events that we may have missed in each others lives.

Like you, we look forward to having our valuable guests at our home and having a meal together is often the highlight of the gathering. Eating with loved ones seems to be one of the enduring pleasures we all look froward too.

Then it is no wonder that Jesus says these amazing words :

'Here I am! I stand at the door and knock. If anyone hears my voice and opens the door, I will come in and eat with that person, and they with me. '

Revelation 3:20

As we honour the people we care for in our lives, do we extend the same honour to Christ's desire to commune with us? He is not just taking about sitting down to an enjoyable meal, but do we give Him a place of honour in our lives?

Jesus is not an intrusive guest. He will never force His way into our home, our lives or our hearts. He waits patiently for an invitation. He knocks politely at the door of our heart.

The question is will we respond and open ourselves to his gentle knock? A lot of times His knocking goes unanswered.

Today let's be hospitable, answer His knock and invite Him into every single area of our lives. His desire is not to judge us but to help us. His desire is to walk with you along your journey and be a constant friend and companion. He will never leave you when you need Him most.

Take a few minutes to pause, mediate and pray.

27

Psalms 103:2-5

"Those who cannot remember the past are condemned to repeat it" George Santayana famously said and it is a truism. When we forget where we came from, we have trouble moving forward. Our past grounds us, but our future redeems us from the grip of its failure.

'Praise the Lord , my soul, and forget not all his benefits– who forgives all your sins and heals all your diseases, who redeems your life from the pit and crowns you with love and compassion, who satisfies your desires with good things so that your youth is renewed like the eagle's.

Psalms 103:2-5

The psalmist looks back at his past state and rejoices in his redeemed state. He acknowledges that there was a defining factor in that redemption. It was the Lord, God who did the redeeming. Not only did He redeem us, He showers us with life, love and liberty. He heals us and gives us a brand new future.

So often we are told to look forward to our great future and it is a remarkable future, and its right that we see all the good things in front of us. However, when we occasionally glance back, we can see where God brought us from. We can appreciate what we have when we see what we were redeemed from.

When I forget to look at my past I feel entitled however, when I remind myself of where God brought me from, I am forever thankful and grateful. I can lift my hands and worship Him. The One who redeemed me, the One who loves me, the One who gives me a better future.

Remind yourself of where God brought you from and you will find it easy to praise God and be thankful for what you do have.

Take a few minutes to pause, mediate and pray.

28

1 Peter 4:10

My wife received a box of chocolates from her friend for her birthday and as soon as she opened the box she offered me, my choice before she took one. Before you think it's all so cute, there is another part to this. If she gets one she does not like, I have to eat it. So I often get chocolates that have a big bite in them!

Peter, however is not not taking about physical gifts from people. He is referring to spiritual gifts that God has given to us. Each of us gets them. These gifts that God gives us are to be used in the service of others.

Each of you should use whatever gift you have received to serve others, as faithful stewards of God's grace in its various forms. '

1 Peter 4:10

Too often we are hesitant to use them, some of us are embarrassed or intimidated or insure. When I first became a Christ follower I was very hesitant to step out in front of people and do what I felt the Lord had asked me to do. I feared the gazes of people and was intimidated by their faces and so I sat down on my gift. This happened until I felt the Lord impress upon me the urgency of what He was asking me to do. In essence He said: "What you have is not yours, it was given to you to share with others. There are people whom I want to bless but are not getting blessed because you are worrying about other people staring at you."

God believes in us and trusts us with a gift so we can be like He is and be a blessing to those around us. As long as we don't use the gifts God has given us we become a dam stopping the outflow of Gods blessing through. When that happens we also don't enjoy the gift He has placed within us.

We are called to be administrators of His gifts in us. Remember He believes in you and the gift He has given you. Take courage and step forward. He is with you and He will always encourage you.

Are you struggling with using your gift? Pray today for strength and courage and let the gift God has given you become to a blessing to others and yourself.

Take a few minutes to pause, mediate and pray.

29

Psalms 28:7

The world's strongest man competition pits some of the worlds most muscular men against each other. They have to perform great feats of strength to outdo each other to claim the tile of World's Strongest Man. We often look on in awe or are fascinated with the performance of these strongmen but they pale in comparison to the strength of our God. He is our ever present help in our times of weakness and trouble.

When we are weak then we are strong, not because we suddenly become endued with super strength, but because the strongest being in the universe is by our side. He is our protector and encourager and He is for us.

When someone tries to belittle us, condemn us or talk down to us, intimidate or criticise us we feel small and insignificant. However, when the God who created the universe stands with us we are not insignificant, nor do we need to feel that way.

He is our defense and our strength. If we learn to lean on Him in our difficult season we can build confidence in His defence of us. When we let His words of encouragement become prominent in our thinking, we find strength to face obstacles and difficulties with new enthusiasm and hope. Our despair can change to joy and our disheartenment can be transformed into a song of triumph!

'The Lord is my strength and my shield; my heart trusts in him, and he helps me. My heart leaps for joy, and with my song I praise him. '

Psalms 28:7

Understand that we all face challenges from time to time. None of us are immune to the ordeals of life, but we can take hope in the knowledge that the Lord who is strong in our defense is also with us in these seasons.

In what area of your life are you facing difficulties? Remind yourself of these words of strength and the promises of His presence to counteract all of the things that come to make you feel weak.

Take a few minutes to pause, mediate and pray.

30

1 John 4:18

Love is the strongest force that exists in the universe. It was the love of God that moved heaven and earth on our behalf. It was love that made Jesus go to the cross. It was love that kept Him nailed to the cross. It was love that kept death from confining Christ to the grave. It is love that called us by name out of darkness and into His light. It was love that gave us life. Love has a name it is Jesus!

When you are in the midst of love there is no room for fear. When you are with the one you love, your signifiant other, you are not afraid. Your emotions of love just overwhelms every other emotion. When you gaze lovingly into their eyes, you are not thinking about the falling economy or a crisis across the world. All you have is “love” in your eyes.

When we look into the loving eyes of God we don’t have to fear for our future, our present or even our past. When we are in a loving relationship with Jesus there is no need to fear the unknown. We can rest in the secure knowledge that no matter what happens, this relationship will endure. As a Christ follower we can be certain that even death cannot destroy our bond with Christ. If we don’t have to fear even death, what do we need to fear if Christ is with us?

The answer is we don't need to fear anything if we are with Christ.

'There is no fear in love. But perfect love drives out fear, because fear has to do with punishment. The one who fears is not made perfect in love. '

1 John 4:18

Rest in the safe knowledge that Jesus holds us in His everlasting arms.

Whatever it is that you are fearful about today? Bring it to Him and let your gaze shift from your circumstance to Him. Let the love of God wash over you and comfort you. You are loved and you can be unafraid.

Take a few minutes to pause, mediate and pray.

31

1 Kings 19:11-13

In todays world we are constantly being bombarded with sound from every direction. There are many ways we feed noise into our lives, television, radio, our phones and other handheld devices. We have to live in a noisy world. Most of us have ear-pods in our ears when we are walking, traveling to and from work and even at home. It has become increasingly challenging to be able to tune out all of the noise and focus in on one thing for any length of time.

I remember when I was a child, my grandfather had an old radio. The kind that had a dial and knobs, you had to turn the dial to tune in to the radio station you wanted to listen to. He loved world news. Through the static and the constant hiss of the radio, he would attempt to get the dial to the exact point to get a clear signal and hear the voice talking hundreds of miles away come in clearly across the airwaves. It took some finesse and time and constant minor adjustments. When it was clear and he was satisfied, he would sit back and listen.

In our world we also have to make an attempt to tune in to God's voice. It's always there, like the man on the broadcast but we need to tune in to the right frequency. We do that by tuning our hearts and minds to His comforting voice. We need to adjust our attention to hear His voice. We need to spend time in stillness and quiet and dull the constant noise to hear Him speak.

In our text today Elijah was running for his life. He thought if he could get as far away from the threat as possible he would be safe. He thought distance would protect him. His mind was filled with his own voice and desperate thoughts.

Finally God stopped him.

'The Lord said, "Go out and stand on the mountain in the presence of the Lord , for the Lord is about to pass by." Then a great and powerful wind tore the mountains apart and shattered the rocks before the Lord , but the Lord was not in the wind. After the wind there was an earthquake, but the Lord was not in the earthquake. After the earthquake came a fire, but the Lord was not in the fire. And after the fire came a gentle whisper. When Elijah heard it, he pulled his cloak over his face and went out and stood at the mouth of the cave. Then a voice said to him, "What are you doing here, Elijah?" '

1 Kings 19:11-13

God wants to speak to us and He wants to speak life into our lives. However, His voice is often eclipsed by what we give our attention to. His voice is gentle and kind and He whispers into our hearts.

Maybe like Elijah we have ended up in a place we don't want to be. Circumstances have forced us into a place we didn't plan to be in. God asked him: What are you doing here, Elijah?

Maybe we should ask ourselves the same question,

Today take some time to tune out all of the noise and adjust our activity to help hear His voice. He wants to speak to you now.

Take a few minutes to pause, mediate and pray.

We hope this devotional has helped you in your faith walk.

About the Author

Gregory J Williams along with his wife lead Transform Church with campuses in Melbourne and Manila

He is a well sought after speaker and leadership coach.

transformchurch.au

www.ingramcontent.com/pod-product-compliance
Lightning Source LLC
LaVergne TN
LVHW052055160826
845678LV00015B/3233